handmade pillows

decorative accents throughout your home

Country Living

handmade pillows

decorative accents throughout your home

Arlene Hamilton Stewart

photographed by Keith Scott Morton

styled by Christine Churchill

foreword by Rachel Newman

HEARST BOOKS NEW YORK

Library of Congress Cataloging-in-Publication data:

Country living handmade pillows : decorative accents throughout your home / by the editors of Country Living.
    p. cm.
    Includes index.
    ISBN 0-688-16134-0
    1. Pillows. 2. Sewing. I. Country living (New York, N.Y.)
TT410.C68 1998
646.2'1--dc21   98-3937
                                  CIP

Printed in Singapore
Text set in Galliard

First Edition
10 9 8 7 6 5 4 3 2 1

www.williammorrow.com

For *Country Living:*
Rachel Newman, Editor-in-Chief
Nancy Mernit Soriano, Editor
Julio Vega, Art Director
John Mack Carter, President, Hearst Magazine Enterprises

Produced by Smallwood & Stewart, Inc., New York City

Art Director: Tomek Lamprecht
Designer: Gretchen Mergenthaler
Editor: Carrie Chase
Illustrator: Ed Lam

table of contents

foreword

I don't think I've ever fallen in love with a room that did not have wonderful pillows. In fact, I often think of pillows as magic accessories. They can create a mood, change a color scheme, and effect a make-over in no time at all. It is a big undertaking to redo a complete room, but a pair of inviting pillows makes a major improvement.

Sewing pillows at home allows you to create exactly what you want, in colors and fabrics of your own choosing—the perfect green to match your bedroom curtains, just the right velvet for your plush sofa. And nothing is a more welcome gift than a handmade pillow—one that invites curling up comfortably with a book, or charms a loved one to sleep with scented potpourri.

Included here are photographs and illustrations for pillows that you will enjoy making. Sewers of all levels (even non-sewers) can explore their creativity and produce versatile and beautiful pillows. One of the great joys of pillows, to me, is that they can be dresed up, dressed down—even easily refashioned on a whim. I have wardrobes of covers for my many, many pillows and switch from one look to another almost as easily as I change the fresh flowers in my apartment. Think of pillows outdoors, too: prop one against a tree to lounge on in the shade, keep half a dozen by the pond or pool, pile them on the glider.

We at *Country Living* hope that this book will inspire even the most needle-wary to explore how much fun pillows can be.

— Rachel Newman, Editor-in-Chief

introduction

Anyone who thinks a pillow is simply a plump object found on a department store shelf is in for a wonderful surprise. There is a world of pillows—with shapes as varied as geometry, and colors, textures, and prints infinitely diverse. Pillows can be anything from diminutive hand-embroidered door hangings to oversize balls. They can be created from costly fabric or from inexpensive muslin. They can become family heirlooms, passed down from generation to generation, or something whipped up to decorate just for the moment. Whatever their shape or size, handmade pillows have more character and individuality, and cost far less, than anything you could purchase.

I've been making pillows all my life. When we were children, my sisters and I would smuggle scraps from Mother's fabric box to make doll pillows, sachets, pin cushions. Years later, we passed along our love of handmade pillows to our own children, and stitched up new ones as fast as the old ones wore out.

The pillows in our homes are not only good-looking, they have personalities to match. Some pillows, like family pets, have become beloved companions: chunky rolls that cuddle sleepy heads, massive reading pillows that support a very healthy habit. Others look after our well-being: Draft dodgers keep our living rooms cozy, aromatherapy pillows fill the air with soothing scents. Pillows even make celebrations more meaningful—felt pillows that remind us of Christmas past—and festive—picnic pillows that say, "Sit down and have fun!"

Pillows are also one of the loveliest and easiest ways to celebrate the change of the seasons—a key-lime green covering announces the arrival of spring as surely as daylight savings time; a stack of velvet and brocade pillows embraces us in front of a blazing hearth in the dead of winter. When the air is filled with honeysuckle and roses, could anything be more summery and inviting than a group of creamy, faded yellows and oxford-cloth blue stripes against a well-worn linen sofa?

More than seasonal mood pieces, pillows are small but powerful design elements with the ability to transform an entire room. A cluster of tartan pillows wakes up a quiet corner of a dark, sophisticated study; a group of muslin squares can ground the bold decor on a sunny veranda. An armload of pillows—in different shapes and sizes, all covered in one vibrant color such as firehouse red—livens up a neutral room better than any expensive rug.

Pillows have so many advantages over other design elements: for one thing, they're versatile and can give any setting a stylish new look without a lot of fuss. Because they're so portable, you can experiment with pillows in different locations. What doesn't work out in one place will surely be successful somewhere else. As a way of previewing ambitious projects, such as slipcovers or curtains, pillows are a sanity saver—you can see how the fabric handles when sewing and how well it launders before making a big design and budget commitment. Best of all, because most pillows require so little fabric, you can make them up with fabric you love—even if it's costly.

Considering how pillows are associated with comfort, it's odd that their history is anything but. For peasant folk, early pillows were mounds of straw (which could well be infested with any number of unpleasant vermin); for the more affluent, hard headrests made from wood, alabaster, and ivory protected their elaborate hairstyles during the night. It wasn't until the late 1800s that the pillow became a serious accessory. It was then that mattresses made of coiled innersprings began to appear in the homes of the middle class, replacing the very expensive down-filled mattress and the much maligned hair-stuffed mattress. This innovation signaled a new image for the bedroom. No longer was it simply a place to sleep—now it became a place to rest. A haven of comfort, the bedroom inspired all sorts of linens and boudoir accessories. Soon, a well-run home featured an assortment of pillows: neck rolls, reading pillows, and sleeping pillows, as well as sofa pillows and chair pillows.

Since our ancestors were by necessity a thrifty lot, they made pillows from all sorts of odd pieces of fabric, giving them the handmade look we so prize today. One of the joys of handmade pillows is that they're easy to do—you don't need a tailor to help you, an advanced degree in sewing, or an expensive electronic sewing machine. We've presented a range of pillows that can be created with different levels of sewing skills. Some require more machine sewing than others—some require no machine stitching at all. Included are pillow ideas for many different occasions and settings along with tips on choosing fabric and trimming, and instructions on cutting and measuring fabric. With so many designs, sizes, and shapes to choose from, there isn't a daybed, chair, love seat, sofa, chaise longue, bed, or even a hammock that should go without a pillow.

— *Arlene Hamilton Stewart*

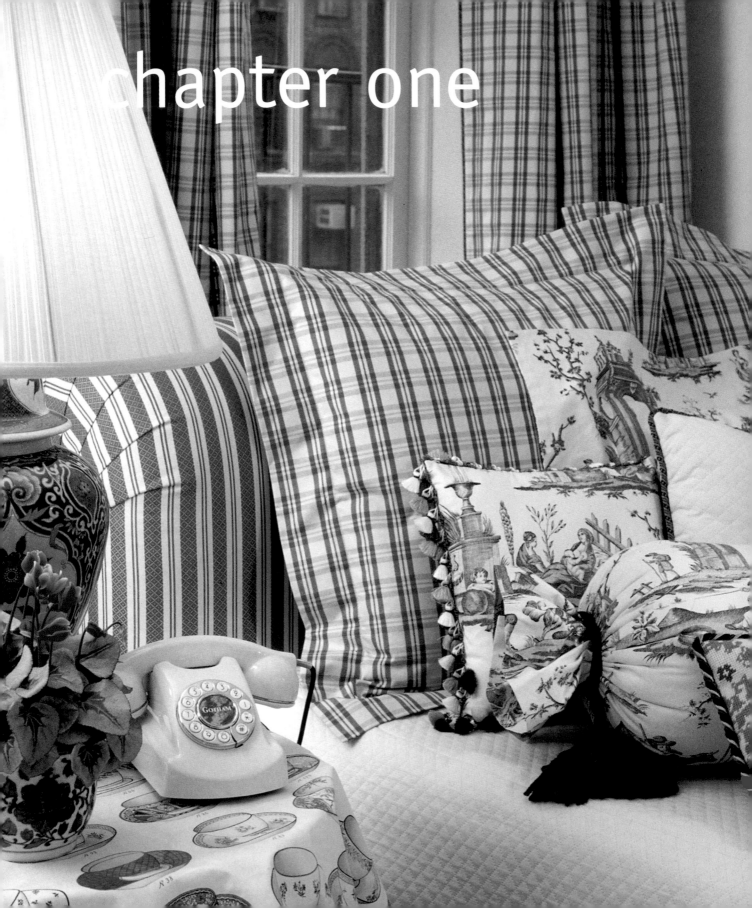

chapter one

pillow shapes & sizes

Two of the first design decisions when making a pillow are shape and size. Pillows go far beyond the familiar square and can be made in virtually any shape and size—hearts, stars, cubes, triangles, and more. Buy conventional shapes in craft and sewing supply stores, or make your own form with muslin and stuffing (see Chapter Five, Materials & Techniques, for how to do this, along with other helpful sewing hints).

When deciding on a pillow size and shape, consider the fabric: Solid-color fabrics offer the most shape options because there is no repeat to be centered. A large pattern works best on an oversize pillow. A heavyweight fabric lends itself to virtually any shape; delicate silk and chiffon need to be lined, which your shape would have to work with. Sometimes details will inspire the shape; perhaps you have four tassels to show off at the corners of a square pillow. Selecting the right size is important to a pillow's appearance so that the finished pillow doesn't seem too massive or too small. But altering a pillow's size—going bigger or smaller than usual—is one way to transform the feel of a room.

Build on the ideas in this chapter—enlarge an oblong; add ball fringe to a circle, piping to a square. Have fun with them.

buttoned-up square

To the simple square, almost anything can be done—embellish each corner with ribbon, sew up the front and back in contrasting fabrics, use as a showcase for a collection of buttons. This ever-charming small square pillow couldn't be easier to make, and there seems to be no end of uses for it: prop a book atop one while reading in bed, nestle a soft square behind a weary neck, or simply tuck one in a chair as a bright color accent.

1. For the pillow back, cut a 10 x 10-inch piece of fabric. For the front, cut one piece 7½ x 10 inches; the other 8 x 10 inches.

2. On the wrong side of the 7½ x 10-inch section, turn in a ½ inch hem along a 10-inch side. Pin and machine stitch along the edge. Remove the pins, then press. Fold this hem in 1 inch to make a piece 6 x 10 inches. Pin and press. Remove the pins.

3. On the wrong side of the 8 x 10-inch panel, turn in a ½-inch hem along a 10-inch side. Pin and machine stitch. Remove the pins, then press.

4. Pin together the right sides of the 10 x 10-inch back and the 6 x 10-inch front, placing the hemmed edge in the middle. Machine stitch a ½-inch seam allowance along the three raw edges. Place the remaining 7½ x 10-inch panel over the other side of the back section, right side down, again with the hemmed edge in the middle. Pin and machine stitch a ½-inch seam allowance along the three sides. Remove the pins. Trim the seams to ¼ inch, slightly clipping the corners to ease the fit.

5. Turn the pillow right side out and poke out the corners. Press.

6. Insert the pillow form. Secure the pillow in the center with pins, then hand sew on a row of buttons, spacing them evenly.

SMALL 5-BUTTON PILLOW:

9-inch pillow form

30 x 10-inch piece fabric

5 buttons

❖   ❖   ❖

sunflower
appliquéd circle

A piece of vintage fabric makes the soft, appealing shape of a circle pillow even more eye-catching. For the appliqué, choose a fabric that has a large single motif, such as this sunflower. Cut the image to include some background, or cut closer to its perimeter. Vary the size and shape of the pillow to coordinate with the center motif.

1. Cut two 15-inch-diameter circles from the cotton; the easiest way to do this is to create a paper pattern with a compass, or to insert a pin in the middle of a piece of paper and attach a pencil to it with a 15-inch length of string. Holding the pencil at the full extent of the string, draw a circle. Use the pattern to cut two circles from the fabric.

2. Cut out the appliqué that you will be using. Pin it to the center of one of the circles. Machine appliqué the motif around the cut edge using a small zigzag stitch, or appliqué by hand with a blanket stitch (see Techniques).

3. Pin the two circles together, right sides facing, leaving an opening for the zipper. At 1 inch above and 1 inch below the zipper opening, stitch a 1/2-inch seam allowance. Remove the pins and press the short seams flat. Baste a 1/2-inch seam allowance between the stitched sections. Pin the closed zipper into the basted seam, easing the curve of the fabric slightly. Baste and sew, using a zipper foot and making sure the zipper teeth are centered between the two seams. Remove the pins.

4. Open the zipper and place the two fabric circles right sides together. Machine stitch a 1/2-inch seam allowance around the remaining circumference. Notch the seam allowance.

5. Turn to the right side and insert the pillow form.

❖   ❖   ❖

14-inch round pillow form

1/2 yard cotton fabric

enough print fabric to cut out one motif

10-inch matching zipper

ball pillow

A ball shape is the most whimsical and original of all. Done in velvet, it brings a sophisticated sense of fun to a space; in a less formal fabric, it would be ideal for a children's room. Stuff this with cotton batting if you can't find a ball form.

1. Cut four oval pieces of velvet in color A and four oval pieces in color B, each $5\frac{7}{8}$ inches wide and $18\frac{1}{2}$ inches long. To cut the ovals, make a paper pattern, drawing the top half of the oval ($5\frac{7}{8}$ x $9\frac{1}{4}$) on the piece of paper, then tracing it onto the folded fabric.

2. To insert the zipper, with right sides together, pin together two ovals in color A. At each end, machine stitch a $\frac{1}{2}$-inch seam allowance, leaving a central opening for the zipper. Baste between the stitched sections. Remove the pins and press the seam open. Lay the closed zipper, face down, along the basted seam. Pin and baste the zipper in place. Remove the pins, then stitch the zipper from the right side of the fabric, using a zipper foot, and stitching $\frac{1}{8}$ inch from the teeth. Carefully remove the basted stitches from the seam and open the zipper.

3. With right sides together, pin together two of the oval sections, making shallow notches in the fabric if necessary to ease the curve. Sew a $\frac{1}{2}$-inch seam allowance along one edge. Remove the pins. Press open the seams. In this way, piece together all of the velvet sections.

4. At the top and bottom of the ball, hand sew a few stitches to bind the oval sections together.

5. Cut two pieces of velvet at least 2 x 2 inches. Follow the package instructions for covering the buttons and attach them to the top and bottom of the ball, hiding the hand-sewn stitches.

6. Insert the pillow form and close the zipper.

15-inch ball form

3/4 yard velvet in color A

3/4 yard velvet in color B

10-inch matching zipper

2 button forms for fabric-covered buttons

❖   ❖   ❖

pillow cases

The rectangular pillowcase is perhaps the most common pillow covering. Until fairly recently, pillowcases were sewn in the home, not manufactured by popular designers. But they are so easy to make, it's almost embarrassing to buy them. Use leftover fabric, and personalize them with prints and colors you really love. Any good quality cotton will wear well. Use this basic pattern to make a queen-size 20 x 30-inch pillow cover. Add trim, lace, or tassels at the opening, or mix and match fabrics. Two yards of fabric makes two pillowcases.

1. Cut two pieces of fabric, 22 x 72 inches long. Working on the wrong side of one piece, turn in a $1/2$-inch hem along a 22-inch side. Pin and press. Remove the pins. Fold in the same edge an additional $2^1/2$ inches, pin, and machine stitch close to the edge. Remove the pins.

2. On the other 22-inch side, also on the wrong side, turn in a $1/2$-inch hem and press. Fold this again $1/2$ inch, pin, and machine stitch in place. Remove the pins and press.

3. Lay the fabric right side up and fold over one end 30 inches. The bottom section will extend by 8 inches (see Illustration). Fold this 8-inch extension back over the top piece. Pin together the two sections and double machine stitch a 1-inch seam allowance along the top and bottom. Remove the pins. Turn the pillowcase right side out and press. Insert a pillow, tucking it under the 8-inch cuff.

4. Make a second pillow with the other 22 x 72-inch piece of fabric.

2 queen-size bed pillows

2 yards fabric

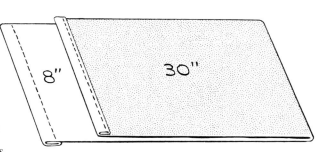

❖   ❖   ❖

oversize reading pillow

Changing the size of a pillow is one way to add interest to a familiar shape. Here, we balloon up a square to create an oversize reading pillow. For anyone who loves to read in bed, or linger on a chaise longue, this large pillow will lend unwavering support. We made it in a pale lime-green linen, but it would be just as lovely in a small floral print or check. Rickrack, one of the most popular trims, provides its own contrasting harmony while slimming down the appearance of this generous pillow.

1. For the zipper section, cut one piece of fabric 3 x 25 inches. Cut another piece, 3½ x 25 inches. Lay both pieces right side down. Fold in a ½-inch hem along the length of each piece, pin, and press. Over the right side of the closed zipper, line up the center of the smaller strip of fabric, right side up, on the edge of the zipper. Pin, baste, and remove the pins. Using a zipper foot, machine stitch from the top to the bottom, close to the zipper opening.

2. Lay the second piece of fabric, right side up, on the other side of the zipper so that it completely covers the middle of the zipper (see Illustration). Pin and machine stitch down the side, close to the zipper opening, and across the bottom. Remove the pins.

24-inch square pillow form (firmer works best here)

2 yards fabric

20-inch matching zipper

1 package (2½ yards) large rickrack

3. Cut two 25-inch squares of fabric for the pillow body. With the right sides together pin the zipper section to the edge of one large piece. Machine stitch a $1/2$-inch seam allowance. Attach to the other large square with the same method. Open the zipper.

4. Cut three strips of fabric for the other sides, 3 x 25 inches each. With the right sides together, pin one 3 x 25-inch piece to a large panel and machine stitch a $1/2$-inch seam allowance. Repeat with the other two side pieces. Press open the seams. At the corners, pin together the raw edges and stitch $1/2$-inch seam allowances. Clip the excess material and corners. Remove the pins.

5. Turn the cover right side out and insert the pillow form. Press the rickrack, then pin it in a large square (ours is 4 inches from edge) and hand sew with small stitches. Remove the pins.

❖   ❖   ❖

ruffled chintz **bolster**

Bolster pillows, or neck rolls, are not as difficult to make as they might look, and they can be made with just one yard of fabric. Use vintage pieces for the tube, or mix and match different patterns, but do opt for lightweight fabrics, which are easier to work with since they don't bulk up. This bolster can be made with or without the ruffle, plain or decorated with braid.

1. Cut out the fabric: For the bolster tube, cut one 17 x 20-inch piece. (If using a print with a repeat, the center should fall in the middle of the 17 x 20-inch piece.) For the end pieces, cut two 12 x 12-inch pieces. For the ruffles, cut two 6½ x 37-inch pieces. For the fabric-covered buttons, cut two pieces at least 2 x 2 inches. Follow the package instructions for covering the buttons.

2. To make the pleated end pieces, use a compass or a pencil with string to draw a circle 12 inches in diameter on both of the 12-inch pieces. Cut out. Then in the center of each circle, draw a 5-inch diameter circle. Cut out the inner circle to form a ring.

3. Around the outer edge of the circles, on the wrong side of the fabric, measure and mark points alternating at 1-inch and ¾-inch intervals. Make pleats by folding the fabric between the ¾-inch marks and pinning each fold under the 1-inch section. Machine stitch a ¼-inch seam allowance along the outside edge. Remove the pins.

6 x 17-inch bolster form

1 yard fabric (if using a print, 1½ yards or more depending on the repeat)

2 button forms for fabric-covered buttons

4. Close the inner rings by folding pleats three and four at a time and tacking them together with basting stitches until all the pleats meet tightly in the middle (see Illustration). Hand sew securely with several stitches, picking up two or three pleats at a time. Sew a fabric-covered button over the raw edges in the middle of each circle.

5. To make the tube, with the right sides together, fold the 17 x 20-inch section in half lengthwise. Pin. Machine stitch a 1-inch seam allowance lengthwise, leaving a 10-inch opening in the middle to insert the pillow form. Remove the pins and press the seams open.

6. To make the ruffles, take each $6^{1}/_2$ x 37-inch section and fold in a 1-inch hem at the $6^{1}/_2$-inch ends. Pin and press flat. Remove the pins. With the right side out, fold each piece in half lengthwise, pin, and sew a $1/_4$-inch seam allowance. Press. On the bottom lengthwise edge of the strip, starting and ending $2^{1}/_4$ inches from the ends, make pleating marks every 2 inches. Fold alternating 2-inch sections together and pin. The pleated strip should measure 19 inches. Machine baste a $1/_2$-inch seam allowance on the raw edge. Press flat.

7. Lay the raw edge of the ruffled section around the perimeter of each end of the inside-out tube. Pin. Machine stitch $3/_8$ inch from the edge. Remove the pins.

8. Keeping the ruffles on the inside of the tube, attach the end section by pinning the right side of the tube to the right side of the end piece (see Illustration). Machine stitch a $5/_8$-inch seam allowance. Remove the pins. Turn the cover right side out and insert the pillow form. Hand sew the opening closed with slip stitches (see Techniques).

❖   ❖   ❖

chapter two

country favorites

Add warmth and charm to your home with a homespun pillow done in the classic country way. In this chapter, you'll find interesting combinations of traditional styles and new fabrics, as well as new uses for some old favorites and reminders of sewing traditions that have fallen by the wayside—like the strawberry pincushion, which is easy to make and a wonderful thing to have at the side of your sewing machine.

We've shaken up traditional Shaker woven seating by applying it to a pillow. This fresh interpretation will perk up a family room or a veranda. And we've played with favorite ginghams and checks, refining the good old country-check seat pad by adding contrasting checkerboard friezes and tiebacks, and putting a mitered-corner ruffle on an oblong pillow.

Because most handmade crafts celebrate the humble, rather than the ornate, we've given you ideas for using the most common of materials in some uncommon ways. Felt holiday pillows have the same handmade feeling as the penny rugs that were so popular in 19th-century New England, while a stack of pillows covered in crisp bandanas couldn't be simpler to make or sweeter looking.

no-sew bandana pillow

There is a certain satisfaction in making a pillow cover without a single stitch. This spiffy cotton pillow is a perfect example of how ingenuity can rise to any occasion. Suppose you're on vacation and the decor in your getaway is less than cheerful—round up a handful of bandanas, a package of rickrack, and a few pillow forms, and within minutes your place and mood are much brighter. Bandanas are such an American classic, they're ideal for anywhere you want informality. Just remember to press the bandanas before beginning.

1. On top of the pillow form, center one bandana, right side up. Pin it in several places to secure. Turn the pillow over and center the right side of the second bandana over the pillow form. Pin in place.

2. Take the ends at one corner in your hand and roll up the excess bandana. Pin the roll in place. Continue rolling on all four sides.

3. Cut the rickrack into four 12-inch lengths.

4. Twist the ends of the bandanas together at each corner and tie them securely with rickrack. Remove the pins.

12-inch pillow form

2 bandanas

1 package (2½ yards) rickrack

❖　❖　❖

country check: mitered ruffle

Fresh checks never lose their appeal. Here, and on the following page, are two simple checked pillows that display different kinds of ruffles—a straight, mitered-corner ruffle and a box-pleat ruffle. Each uses two different yet related fabrics, one for the pillow and the other for the ruffle.

1. To make the pillow insert, pin together the two pieces of muslin, right sides facing. Sew a ¹/₂-inch seam allowance around three sides, remove the pins, and turn right side out. Insert the cotton batting and sew the opening closed with slip stitches. For the pillow body, cut two pieces of 10 x 28-inch fabric, centering the checks.

2. For the mitered ruffle, cut two 7 x 17-inch strips and two 7 x 35-inch strips from the second fabric, centering the checks. Fold each strip in half lengthwise, wrong sides together. Press each strip to mark the fold. Open up one strip and lay it flat, wrong side facing up. At one end fold each corner toward the center fold line, making a point. Press to mark the folds. Repeat at the other end. Cut along the short folds to make points at each end. Repeat for the remaining strips.

3. Pin the strips, corner to corner, right sides together. Stitch ¹/₂ inch from the edge along the sides of each corner. Turn the border inside out, poking out the corners, and press. Lay the border on top of the pillow body with the raw edges aligning and the border facing toward the inside of the pillow, pin, and baste. Remove the pins.

4. Making sure the ruffle stays positioned inside the case, place the pillow back over the front, right sides facing. Sew in the zipper as on page 37, step 5, then open the zipper and sew the remaining three sides.

5. Turn the case right side out, insert the pillow form, and zip closed.

two 10 x 28-inch pieces muslin

1 yard checked fabric for body

2¹/₂ yards coordinated fabric for ruffle

loose cotton batting

12-inch matching zipper

❖   ❖   ❖

country check: box pleats

1. Cut two 15-inch squares of fabric for the pillow front and back, centering the fabric checks. From the second fabric, cut a strip 7 x 72 inches for the ruffle, centering the fabric checks.

2. Pin together the short ends of the ruffle strip with the right sides facing and sew a $1/2$-inch seam allowance. Remove the pins and press the seam open. Turn the ruffle right side out and fold it in half, to make a $3^1/2$-inch wide loop of fabric. Pin and machine stitch a $1/4$-inch seam allowance along the long edge. Remove the pins.

3. Place the ruffle against the right side of the pillow front, with the raw edges together. Begin at the center of each side and arrange the ruffle into three loose box pleats along each edge. To make the box pleats, fold the fabric into itself on both sides of each pleat. If your fabric is checked, try to make sure each boxed section has the same pattern. Adjust the pleat depth until the ruffle fits the size of the pillow, then pin and baste $1/4$ inch from the raw edges.

5. Making sure the ruffle stays positioned inside the case, place the pillow back over the front, right sides facing. At each end of one side, pin and machine sew a $1/2$-inch seam allowance through all three layers, leaving a central opening to insert the zipper. Remove the pins. Machine baste along the seam in which the zipper is to be inserted. Press the seam open. Pin and baste the closed zipper to the wrong side of the seam, making sure that the zipper is centered over the seam. Remove the pins. On the right side of the fabric, using a zipper foot, stitch along both sides and ends of the zipper. Remove the basting stitches.

6. Open the zipper and machine sew the remaining three sides.

7. Turn the case right side out, insert the pillow form, and zip closed.

❖   ❖   ❖

14-inch square pillow form

$1/2$ yard checked fabric for pillow body

2 yards coordinated fabric for ruffle

10-inch matching zipper

pin cushion

Pins and needles—we still use them, and lose them. Every sewer needs a pincushion to stay organized. Recreating this charming helper is both practical and evocative. A pincushion is, in essence, a miniature pillow. However, it is best stuffed with sand rather than batting to hold the pins and needles securely (sand also helps keep tips sharp). Ours is a strawberry, a simple shape to make, but consider a slice of watermelon or an orange with a few leaves at the top.

1. To make the inside case, cut a 10-inch-diameter circle from the muslin using a compass or pencil with string. Fold the muslin in half, then in half again, to make a cone shape. Machine stitch a $^1/2$-inch seam allowance along the short straight edge. Hand sew a row of loose running stitches $^1/4$ inch from the top edge. Begin to gather the stitches while filling the shape with sand. When filled, pull the gathered top closed and poke the gathers down into the cone. Hand sew back and forth over the gathered closure to make the top leakproof.

2. Make another cone shape from the red fabric and seam the same way. Cover the muslin cone with the red cone and fold the fabric into little pleats at the top, cutting away any excess. Hand sew short running stitches to secure the top pleats.

3. Cut a 5-inch-diameter circle from the green fabric. Cut six leaves into the edge of the circle. Place the leaf circle over the red cone and pin it in a few spots to secure. Hand sew the edges of the leaves to the body of the pincushion, turning the edges under by about $^1/16$ inch as you sew. Remove the pins.

❖   ❖   ❖

sand for stuffing
  (available at craft stores)

10-inch square muslin

10-inch square red cotton

6-inch square green cotton

woven shaker pillow

This simple pillow is based on a traditional woven Shaker chair seat. You can use any two contrasting colors of fabric tape (the tape is available through Shaker workshops), or strips of any fabric or ribbon. The webbing is heavy, so choose a sturdy fabric such as canvas for the pillow back.

1. Cut an 18-inch square of canvas for the pillow backing.

2. Cut the webbing into 18-inch strips, eight of each color.

3. To weave the pillow top, it is helpful to have a pinning board (or a large sheet of foam core) to secure the strips with pins as you weave. Lay out three vertical strips of one color webbing. Weave in three horizontal strips of the contrasting webbing, under and over, forming a checkerboard pattern. Make sure each strip is tucked snugly next to the adjoining one. Place a pin through the end of each strip into the board as you weave. Continue weaving and adding strips until all the strips have been used.

4. Baste all around the weaving, about ¼ inch from the edge, to keep the strips in position.

5. Pin the two pillow pieces together, right sides facing. Sew a ¾-inch seam allowance all around, leaving space to insert the pillow form. Remove the pins.

6. Turn the case right side out, insert the pillow form, and hand sew the opening closed with slip stitches (see Techniques).

❖   ❖   ❖

16-inch square pillow form

½ yard canvas

4 yards each two colors of 1-inch cotton webbing

pinning board or foam core (optional)

felt christmas
pillow

Richly colorful, festive felt is often associated with the winter holidays: Felt stockings, table runners, and tree skirts blaze with holiday trimmings. Available in a dazzling spectrum of colors, felt cuts like no other material, beautifully holding an edge. A stack of felt pillows, each with a different border, is a quick and inexpensive way to endow a family room or dining area with the holiday spirit.

1. Cut two 17½-inch squares of felt. Make a pattern for the body and scalloped border: From the construction paper, cut a 17½-inch square. Draw a second square 1¾ inches in from the edges. With a compass draw a row of four circles, each 3½ inches in diameter, side by side along each edge. Cut along the edge of the top halves of the circles, around the whole pattern (see Illustration). Pin together the felt squares and center the pattern on top. Pin the pattern to the felt and cut around each edge. Remove the pattern and the pins.

2. Remove the top piece of felt and center the pillow form on the bottom piece. Center the top piece on the form and pin tightly around the form and scalloped edge. Cut a long length of embroidery thread and separate out two strands. Thread a needle and secure each scallop to the pillow form with three decorative stitches.

3. With embroidery floss make a blanket stitch (see Techniques) all around the scallops. Remove the pins.

SCALLOPED FELT PILLOW
WITH BLANKET-STITCH BORDER:

12-inch pillow form

½ yard felt

heavy construction paper

1 skein embroidery floss

❖   ❖   ❖

tieback cushion

The charm of this simple seat cushion lies in the fact that the ties become part of the design. Two long strips of the same fabric, cut on the bias, are sewn along each side the length of the cushion, ending in the ties that secure the cushion to the back of the chair. Clever, too, is the fact that the base fabric wraps around both sides of the case, making the amount of fitting and sewing minimal. You will want to adjust the measurements of this pattern to suit the seat size of your chair. Keep in mind, especially, that the position of the strips should be adjusted so the ties are where you will attach them to the chair.

1. To make the cushion insert, cut a piece of batting 17 x 34 inches. Cover both sides of the foam with the batting; loosely baste to hold in place. Cut a 19 x 35-inch piece of muslin, fold it in half, pin, and sew a $1/2$-inch seam allowance along three sides. Remove the pins. Turn right side out and insert the foam. Fold under and sew up the remaining seam by hand or machine.

2. Cut a 17 x 34-inch piece of checked fabric for the cushion body. Cut two $2^{1}/_{2}$ x 17-inch strips for the sides.

3. For the ties, on the bias, cut two 4 x 60-inch pieces of fabric. Fold the long edges in half, right sides together. Pin and machine stitch a $1/2$-inch seam allowance to make long tubes. Remove the pins. Turn the tubes right side out (attach a large safety pin to one end of the tube, poke the pin end inside the tube, and use the pin to help get the tube turned inside out).

4. Press the ties flat with the center seam hidden to the underside of each tube. Fold about $1/2$ inch of fabric in on each end of the ties and sew across to secure.

16-inch square piece $1^{1}/_{2}$-inch wide foam

17 x 34-inch piece batting

$3/4$ yard muslin

3 yards checked fabric

5. Fold the short end of the cushion fabric in about $\frac{1}{4}$ inch toward the wrong side of the fabric. Fold in another 1 inch, press and pin. Machine sew very close to the folded edge. Repeat at the other end. Remove the pins.

6. Position the ties on the seat fabric about 3 inches from each side (or whatever distance suits your chair). Pin and carefully machine sew the ties to the fabric, working as closely as possible to the edges of the ties. Remove the pins.

7. Fold one short end of each side piece in about $\frac{1}{4}$ inch toward the wrong side of the fabric. Fold in another 1 inch, press and pin. Machine sew close to the folded edge. Remove the pins and press. With wrong sides facing out, pin the side pieces to the main piece with the seamed ends overhanging by about 1 inch. Sew a $\frac{1}{2}$-inch seam allowance all around. Remove the pins. Fold over the 1-inch overhangs and slip stitch the ends to the fabric.

8. Turn the cover right side out, insert the pillow, and tie it to the chair.

❖ ❖ ❖

seat cushions

A lovely variation of the square tie-back cushion, perfect for café-style chairs, is a circle shape. Make a welt—a strip of fabric for the side between the top and bottom—and attach the circular pieces of fabric to it. Piping on the seams gives these a very finished look. If you plan on using the cushions outdoors, make these in a waterproof fabric to protect them from a chance rain shower.

lace sham

This pillow classic has a flap closure in the middle of the back rather than being open at one end like a pillowcase. Deep eyelet lace makes a simple ruffled pillow sham. Vary the design by the choice of lace ruffle—old or new, the texture of the fabric, or by mixing different colors and tones. Adjust the measurements of the sham for your pillow.

1. Cut one piece of fabric for the front, 25 x 18 inches.

2. Cut two pieces of fabric for the back, 18 x 16 inches each. On the wrong side of the fabric, turn in a 1/2-inch hem on one of the 18-inch edges of each piece and press. Turn in another 1/2 inch, press, pin, and machine stitch close to the edge. Remove the pins.

3. With right sides facing up and the hemmed edge in the middle, overlap the two back pieces by 5 inches so that they are the same size as the front piece. Pin and set aside.

4. Make the ruffle by sewing a loose running stitch along the lacing, 1/4 inch from the inner edge (see Illustration). Sew a second row of running stitches 1/4 inch from the first. Pulling gently on the threads, loosely gather the ruffle and place it on the pillow front edge, right sides facing and the raw edges together. Adjust the gathers until the ruffle fits the front. Pin and sew a 1/4-inch seam allowance all around. Remove the pins.

5. Pin the back and front together, right sides facing. Sew a 1/2-inch seam allowance all around. Remove the pins.

6. Turn the sham right side out and insert the pillow through the flapped closure.

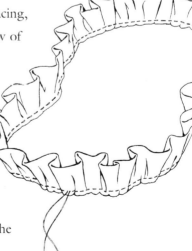

standard down-filled bed pillow

1 yard cotton fabric

5 yards eyelet edging, about 4 inches deep

❖   ❖   ❖

chapter three

the gift pillow

The pillow you give is probably the most fun to make: Most likely you'll work with lovely materials, and get to try out new ideas. For my niece Sarah's first apartment, I wanted to give her something special. A handmade pillow with an elaborate "S" embroidered in cross-stitch was the perfect answer. It evokes the look of intricate samplers from the late 1800s, but with infinitely less work. This elegant pillow certainly has more lasting value than store-bought housewares.

In this chapter, we've made suggestions for all sorts of gift pillows, some that are perfect for the home, others that are perfect for the person. An aromatherapy pillow, scented with the recipient's favorite fragrance, would be an ethereal bedside companion. Like the draft dodger and the picnic mat, this pillow goes to work—it's practical as well as thoughtful.

For a house-warming or an anniversary, there is the undisputed elegance of velvet and damask, equally luxurious in the bedroom or the living room. One attribute of a pillow made in sections like this is its economy—it requires only small pieces of sumptuous materials. And the work that you put into making something by hand will be appreciated forever.

cross-stitch pillow

Cross-stitch is found in examples of folk art dating back to the 16th century. In the 1800s a young American girl would spend many productive hours stitching samplers that demonstrated her skill with a needle. With its charm and character, cross-stitch is a graphic way to commemorate family milestones and celebrate happy occasions. The initial in this pillow was copied from a sampler from the late 19th century and worked on a sepia-colored cross-stitch canvas.

1. Design an initial (or another design) in the center of a piece of graph paper, allowing one square to represent each stitch.

2. If you plan to use transfer paper, make an "X" across each square of the graph paper, to represent one stitch. Center the transfer paper wherever you want the design to fall on the cross-stitch canvas, and copy the design. If you are using more than one color floss, color each square with a colored pencil accordingly. Using the basic cross-stitch (see Illustration), follow the design.

3. You can also simply use the graph paper as a guide, eyeing it as you stitch directly onto the canvas. This is easier than it seems. Cross-stitch canvas is an open, even grid, allowing you to easily count stitches. Decide how many thread intersections in the grid will represent each stitch. Locate the center of your fabric, match it with the center of the graph paper, and using the basic cross-stitch, follow the design.

11-inch square pillow form

one piece cross-stitch canvas (15 x 18 inches is a common size and unfolded is best)

1/2 yard velvet or backing material

1 1/3 yards piping cord, medium-width

1 skein embroidery floss

embroidery needle

graph paper

transfer paper (optional, from a craft store)

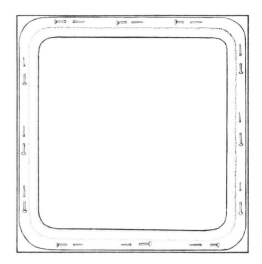

4. Make the piping. While piping is traditionally made from strips of fabric cut on the bias, most new velvet is elastic enough to fit corners. Cut a strip of velvet 2 x 45 inches. On the wrong side, fold in 1 inch at both short ends. Pin and press. Remove the pins. Lay the velvet wrong side up and place the cord in the middle lengthwise, leaving a 1-inch fabric overlap at one end. Fold the fabric over the cord lengthwise, pin, and with a zipper foot machine stitch close to the cord. Remove the pins. Take both ends and make a circle. Tuck the cord inside the overlap and stitch across the joint.

5. Cut an 11¾-inch square of velvet for the backing. On the right side of the fabric, pin the piping around the perimeter of the square, raw edges together, and machine stitch in place (see Illustration). Pin together the right sides of the embroidered canvas and the velvet backing, and machine stitch a seam all around near the piping, leaving at least a 6-inch space to insert the pillow form. Trim the excess fabric from the seams and turn right side out.

6. Insert the pillow form and sew the opening closed with slip stitches (see Techniques).

❖   ❖   ❖

embroidery floss

Embroidery floss has six strands of thread per skein. Cut a length and separate the strands into the weight you prefer—two, three, four, or use all strands. When you hand-embroider, an embroidery hoop will help keep the stitch tension even.

roll-up picnic mat

Celebrate summer by making a roll-up mat for your favorite picnic-going companion. Padded or unpadded, this oversize pillow makes a handy sit-upon for picnicking on the shore, at a concert or tailgate, or in front of the fireplace. And it's a cinch to carry, rolled up and fastened with its ties. Vary the size and fabric according to your desires. We loved the perkiness of this classic cotton tablecloth fabric, although you could use oil cloth or awning material for a damp-resistant pillow. The muslin-covered pillow insert is removable for laundering.

1. For the pillow insert, cut a piece of batting 25 x 50 inches. Fold it in half to make a 25-inch square. Cut two 26-inch squares of muslin. Pin together and machine sew a $1/2$-inch seam allowance around all four sides, leaving a gap to insert the batting. Turn the muslin case right side out, insert the batting, then close up the gap with slip stitches (see Techniques).

2. For the mat body, cut two pieces of fabric, 28 x 33 inches each. On the wrong side of each piece, fold in a 1-inch hem on a short end. Pin and press. Remove the pins, then fold this edge in 2 inches. Pin and machine stitch close to the folded inside edge. Press and remove the pins.

3. For the ties, cut a 4 x 36-inch piece of fabric. Cut this in half lengthwise to make two strips, 36 x 2 inches each, then fold these in half widthwise and cut to create four strips, 2 x 18 inches each. On the wrong sides, fold in a 1-inch hem at each short end. Press flat. Fold the long edges in half, right sides together. Pin and machine stitch a $1/4$-inch seam allowance to make long tubes. Remove the pins. Turn the tubes right side out (attach a large safety pin to one end of the tube, poke the pin end inside the tube, and use the pin to help get the tube turned inside out). Press.

1 yard fabric, 60 inches wide

1$1/2$ yards white muslin, 36 inches wide

1$1/2$ yards batting

8 buttons (optional)

4. To assemble the body, place the two pieces wrong side out with the folded edges together. Pin and machine stitch a 1-inch seam allowance along the two long edges. Remove the pins. Press the seams open. Then close up the unhemmed short end by machine stitching a 1-inch seam allowance.

5. At the top, turn the edges over 2 inches onto the inside. Pin and machine stitch close to the folded inside edge. Remove the pins. Turn right side out and press.

6. Pin the ties on the right side of the fabric at a distance of 5 inches from each corner and 2 inches below the edge. Make sure the opposing ties line up. Attach with a few secure stitches. Remove the pins. Hand sew buttons on each side to hide stitches if you wish.

7. Insert muslin pillow, tie, and go!

❖   ❖   ❖

seat-saver

Change the dimensions and fabric of this pillow for a mat that your bottom will love come a chilly fall day at the football game. Cut a 10-inch wide, 40-inch long rectangle out of fleece for the mat body— big enough for two people. Sew the ties to the short end and carry the mat into the stadium along with a thermos of hot chocolate.

draft dodger

When Jack Frost rattles at the windowpane, and nippy drafts send one scurrying for snug slipper socks, there's nothing cozier or more practical than a draft dodger pillow. Show your consideration for people living in cold climes with this easy-to-make gift. Long tubes filled with a heavy material such as dried beans, draft dodgers stand on duty protecting windows and doorways from uninvited Arctic breezes. Using wool fabric adds an additional feeling of warmth to a room.

1. On the wrong side, turn in the short ends of the fabric $1\frac{1}{2}$ inches. Pin and press. Remove the pins. Fold in half lengthwise, right sides together, and pin the raw edges together. Double machine stitch a $\frac{1}{2}$-inch seam allowance. Remove the pins and turn right side out.

2. Cut the ribbon into two 12-inch sections. Tie a piece of ribbon tightly around one pillow end. Fill the tube with beans until it's as bulky as you like. Tie the remaining end.

12 x 36-inch piece fabric

1 to 2 pounds dried beans for stuffing

24 inches ribbon

❖   ❖   ❖

beaded ties

For a rustic look, you can tie off the draft dodger with braid (you'll need about 3 yards) and wooden beads (four, with large drill holes). Cut the braid in half and tie it twice around one end of the pillow, about 2 inches from the end. Double knot, then fill the tube with beans. Tie the remaining end. A few inches above the tie, make a triple knot, insert a bead, and triple knot again. Repeat for all four strands of the braid. Trim the ends where desired.

quilted aromatherapy **pillow**

Sweet dreams are assured in the relaxing company of an aromatherapy pillow. Many people believe that flowers, plants, herbs, and other botanicals possess healing properties. Among the most soothing botanicals is thought to be lavender. Our little pillow is quilted with separate areas for lavender, potpourri, or any filling you desire. Pop it on the bed in the morning, and by the time you retire, its soft fragrance should escort you into a most restful slumber.

1. Cut two 10-inch squares of the muslin. Cut three 10-inch squares of the dotted Swiss. (Dotted Swiss has a right side and a wrong side; the right side is sharper in detail.) With the right side out, pin one of the dotted Swiss squares to a muslin square and machine stitch ¼ inch from the edge. Attach together another square of dotted Swiss and muslin in the same way.

2. On the muslin side of one muslin/dotted Swiss square, with a pencil mark ½ inch in from all the outer edges and, with a ruler, draw connecting lines. Then from the first ruler mark, mark off 3 inches along each side. With the ruler, connect the marks in light lines.

3. Lay the square, dotted Swiss side up, and place the remaining piece of dotted Swiss on top, right side up. Pin together securely to prevent fabric from shifting. Turn over and machine sew only those lines marked "A" (see Illustration). Remove the pins.

⅓ **yard white muslin**

⅓ **yard dotted Swiss or organdy**

four 7-inch squares polyester batting (additional for stuffing, optional)

herbal filling

2 yards plus 1 inch braid trimming

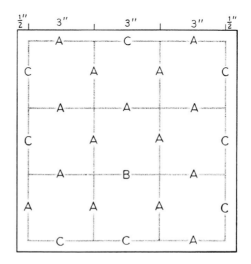

4. Insert a paper tube, such as a cardboard paper towel roll, through opening "B," and fill the enclosure with botanical material. Pin and machine stitch seam "B." Using the same method, fill and sew all openings marked "C" until all nine squares are completed. Remove the pins.

5. Pin the two pieces together, right sides facing, and sew a $^1/_2$-inch seam allowance all around, leaving space to insert the batting. Remove the pins. Turn the case right side out and carefully insert the batting, making sure it lies smooth. Fill the cavity with additional shredded batting for a plumper pillow if desired. Close the opening with slip stitches (see Techniques).

6. Cut strips of trimming to cover the stitching across the front. Pin and hand sew in place. Pin the trimming around the perimeter of the pillow and sew in place, hiding the raw edges where two ends meet. Remove the pins.

❖ ❖ ❖

potpourri

For truly homemade aromatherapy pillows, grow and dry your own herbs and flowers. Lavender counters insomnia; lilac has an intoxicating aroma that lulls people—especially children—to sleep, as does the old-fashioned biennial purple or white sweet rocket (also known as vesper flower). Pick your flowers or herbs in late morning, after the dew has evaporated, and hang them in bunches upside down in a cool, well-ventilated, dark spot until they are fully dry. Crumble them gently between your fingers.

gardener's pocket pillow

This whimsical pillow features a pocket sewn into a terra-cotta pot; slip a little gift for a gardener into it. Choose a soft fabric such as a corduroy for the back and a stiffer fabric for the pots, such as cotton canvas. You could also use ultrasuede, felt, or leather. Some details were painted on the pot (using fabric paint), but you could use embroidery stitches instead, or just leave it plain.

1. Cut two 17-inch squares of brown fabric for the pillow.

2. Make a paper pattern of the pot front, copying and enlarging it from the photograph to create a pot about 10 inches wide and 10 inches tall; add an extra 1½ inches to the top of the shape for the lip of the pot. Use the pattern to cut out a piece of terra-cotta fabric. Cut a 10 x 4-inch oval for the back of the pot.

3. Pin the oval forming the pot back to the center of the right side of one 17-inch square, about 3 inches from the top. Embroider by machine or by hand around the edge of the oval. If sewing by hand, use a blanket stitch (see Techniques) or a zigzag stitch.

4. Fold in the top of the pot front about 1½ inches toward the wrong side, to create the lip of the pot. For added detail, stitch across the raw edge of the lip, from the right side. Place the pot on the oval, aligning the two edges. Pin in place. Embroider by machine or by hand along the sides and bottom of the pot, but not across the top (this forms the pocket). Remove the pins.

5. Pin the two pillow pieces together, right sides facing. Sew a ½-inch seam allowance all around, leaving space to insert the pillow form. Remove the pins.

6. Turn the case right side out, insert the pillow form, and sew closed the opening with slip stitches.

❖   ❖   ❖

LARGE PILLOW:

16-inch square pillow form

½ yard brown fabric

¼ yard terra-cotta-colored fabric

construction paper

brown embroidery thread

painted pillowcase

Pillowcases can be personalized with paint, done for a friend in her favorite colors or painted by children as a charming gift to give their grandparents. Fabric paints, readily available from craft stores, are easy to use and the results are durable and washable. The paints can be applied to store-bought 100% cotton pillowcases and bedsheets. Here, a stencil pattern decorates the edges. You can purchase stencil patterns or trace an interesting pattern from a book or magazine onto acetate. Another option is to simply draw your own design.

1. Create a motif (like the one shown here), or use a stencil, and enlarge it so that it fits comfortably along the edge of your pillow.

2. Copy the pattern to the stencil paper. Carefully cut the stencil out with an X-Acto knife.

3. Lightly trace the pattern onto the pillowcase with pencil.

4. Fill in the pattern using a brush and fabric paint. Let dry.

white cotton pillowcase

fabric paints

paintbrush

thick paper for stencil

X-Acto knife

❖   ❖   ❖

variations

For a less even look you could cut the stencil from acetate and use a stencil brush to apply the paint. Tape the stencil to your pillowcase. Work from the edge of the design toward the center, being careful that the paint does not seep under the stencil edges.

velvet & damask pillow

The combination of lush velvet and satiny damask conjures up castles and country manor houses. This pillow, which has as its focal point an unusual large-scale damask pattern, is regal and formal, yet easy to make. A variation of this pillow would be to make velvet "tubing" to create a frame around a center panel. (Make a tube by cutting a 2-inch wide strip of velvet long enough to go around the panel, fold with the right sides facing, and sew a 1/4-inch seam from the edge. Turn the tube right side out and stitch on as desired to decorate the front.) Whatever design you opt for, choose fabrics that have similar tones.

1. To make an overlap closure on the back, cut two 17 x 12-inch pieces of velvet. On the wrong side, turn in a 1/2-inch hem on one 17-inch edge of each piece and press. Turn the edges in another 1/2 inch, press, pin, and machine stitch close to the edge. Remove the pins.

2. With the right sides facing up and the hemmed edges on the inside, overlap the two back pieces by 5 inches so that they create one 17 x 17-inch piece. Pin together along the hemmed edges and set aside.

3. Cut two pieces of velvet for the front sides, 17 x 6 inches each. Cut a piece of damask for the front center, 17 x 7 inches. Pin the long edges of the velvet side pieces to the damask, right sides together. Sew a 1/2-inch seam allowance. Remove the pins, turn the side panels outward, and press the seams open.

4. Pin the front to the back, right sides together, with the back opening vertical. Sew a 1/2-inch seam allowance all around. Remove the pins.

5. Turn the case right side out and insert the pillow form. Sew the opening closed with slip stitches (see Techniques.)

THREE-PANEL PILLOW:

16-inch square pillow form

1/2 yard velvet

1/4 yard damask

❖ ❖ ❖

chapter four

old fabrics, new pillows

Long ago, people had to be thrifty, saving every precious scrap of fabric and recycling it into useful objects. What wasn't incorporated into quilts and bedding was used for rugs. Today we're surrounded by abundance—we no longer have to weave fabrics or wait for traveling peddlers to arrive with bolts of enticing goods. A trip to the nearest mall reveals riches our ancestors couldn't possibly have imagined. Still, a certain satisfaction exists in creatively transforming the old into the new, and that's what this chapter is devoted to.

Here you'll find suggestions for preserving and revitalizing the past, along with hints on how to render old fabric anew with the proper care. The designs are versatile and can be interpreted in many different ways, and you'll see variations made by combining vintage pieces with new fabrics.

Old objects often have a depth of detail not found in new. For example, we've mimicked the warmth and patina of an Aubusson rug by piecing together antique damask and trim, and highlighted the exquisite detailing of a beloved but worn chenille bedspread, now made into soft pillows.

aubusson pillow

This lush pillow takes its inspiration from the soft patterns of an antique Aubusson rug. Indeed, you could make the pillow from rug scraps if you have a heavy-duty sewing machine. But our version uses damask fabric and ribbon to achieve the same effects. Choose one damask fabric with a center motif that can be cut out to form the centers of the pattern blocks. The two other damask fabrics can have a more random pattern. Somewhat like working with quilt pieces, you will make three pattern blocks attached and framed with damask ribbon.

1. To make the pillow insert, pin together the two pieces of muslin, right sides facing. Sew a $1/2$-inch seam allowance around three sides, remove the pins, and turn right side out. Insert the cotton batting and sew the opening closed with slip stitches.

2. For the pillow back, cut a $22^1/2$ x $8^1/2$-inch piece of pattern A damask.

3. For the pillow front, you will make three pattern blocks. To make a pattern block: Cut a $6^1/2$-inch square of pattern A. Cut a $4^3/4$-inch square of pattern B. Cut a $2^3/4$-inch square center motif from pattern C. Fold in the edges of the two smaller pieces $1/4$ inch to the wrong side and press. Lay the three squares one on top of another, placing the two smaller pieces as diamonds at a 45° angle. Pin in place. Carefully machine sew around each block as close as possible to the edge. Remove the pins. Repeat to make two more pattern blocks.

4. Cut two 10-inch lengths of ribbon. Lay a piece of ribbon overlapping the edges of two pattern blocks by $1/4$ inch. Make sure the ribbons are centered, with an equal amount left extra at each end. Pin and sew close to the edge of the ribbon. Attach the third pattern block in the same way. Remove the pins.

two 22 x 8-inch pieces muslin

$3/4$ yard pattern A damask fabric

$1/4$ yard pattern B damask fabric

$1/4$ yard pattern C damask fabric, with a center motif

$2^1/2$ yards of $1^1/2$-inch wide damask ribbon

loose cotton batting for insert

2 yards tassel fringe

5. Cut two 25-inch lengths of ribbon and two more 10-inch lengths of ribbon to frame the pillow. Place the ribbon along the edge of the attached pattern blocks. The ribbon should overlap the piece by about $1/4$ inch all around. Pin the ribbon. Fold under and miter the corners. To miter corners, crease from the corner to the outside edge, creating a triangular flap of fabric. Check that this is a 45° angle with a draftman's triangle. Stitch from the inner corner to the outer corner, then trim the seam edges. Slip stitch along the diagonal at the corner to secure. Sew the ribbon to the pattern blocks as close to the ribbon edge as possible. Remove the pins.

6. Place the fringe around the edge of the pillow front, tassel side facing toward the inside of the pillow. Pin and sew the fringe about $1/4$ inch from the raw edge. Remove the pins.

7. Pin the front and back pillow pieces together, right sides facing. Make sure the tassels stay inside the pillow. Sew a $1/2$-inch seam allowance all around, leaving one short end open to insert the pillow form. Remove the pins.

8. Turn the case right side out, insert the pillow form, and sew closed the opening with slip stitches (see Techniques).

❖　　❖　　❖

bark cloth pillow

Bark cloth, a heavy weave of cotton with tropical floral designs, once so popular for covering the cushions of rattan and porch furniture, is now prized by fabric enthusiasts for its wonderful pastel colors and flora and fauna patterns. Bark cloth is casual glamour, recalling cooling tropic breezes and swaying palms. It can still be found in antiques stores, upscale flea markets, and from linen dealers, although you might have to cut up an existing cushion or curtain. This pillow is framed on the front with a coordinating color of ticking fabric; a second ticking color is used for the pillow back and the piping.

1. Cut a 21-inch square of ticking fabric color A for the pillow back. Cut an 18-inch square of the bark cloth for the pillow front. In the four corners of the pillow front, mark a dot $1/2$ inch in from the edges.

2. Make the piping (see Techniques) out of ticking color A. Cut $1^1/2$-inch strips of fabric on the bias; join enough strips to make 90 inches of piping. Lay the ticking wrong side up and place the cord in the middle lengthwise. Fold the fabric over the cord lengthwise, pin, and machine stitch with a zipper foot close to the cord. Remove the pins.

3. Cut four 3 x 21-inch strips of ticking color B on the bias, to make a border for the bark cloth. On the end of each strip, mark a dot that is $1^1/2$ inches in from the short edge and $1/2$ inch from the long edge.

4. Lay one of the strips along the edge of the bark cloth with right sides facing. Match the dots on each strip with the dots on the corners of the bark cloth. Pin to secure. Repeat with the other strips (the strips will overlap at the corners). Sew each strip individually with a $1/2$-inch seam allowance, beginning and ending at the corner dots. Where the strips overlap, miter the corners: Crease from the stitched corner to

20-inch square pillow form

$1/2$ yard bark cloth

$1^1/2$ yards of color A cotton ticking

$1/2$ yard of color B cotton ticking

8 feet cotton cording

the outside edge, creating a triangular flap of fabric. Check that this is a 45° angle with a draftman's triangle. Stitch from the inner corner to the outer corner, then trim the seam edges. Remove the pins. Fold the ticking frame out and press.

5. Position the cording facing inward along the edge of the right side of the pillow front, starting at the center of one of the sides. Pin (and baste if necessary) all around. Where the cording meets, cut so there is a ½-inch overlap. Open one end of the cording fabric about ½ inch and clip a ½ inch of the cording inside. Fold over the end of the fabric about ¼ inch and reposition the cording so it encloses the raw other end of cording. This makes a tidy cording join.

6. Pin the two pillow pieces together, right sides facing. Sew around the edge using a ½-inch seam allowance all around, leaving space to insert the pillow form. Remove the pins.

7. Turn the case right side out, insert the pillow form, and sew closed the opening with slip stitches.

❖   ❖   ❖

vintage bedspread pillow

It's always hard to part with beautiful linens—even when they're worn or stained. Chenille has a luxurious quality, and if you're lucky enough to own a chenille bedspread, or to discover one at a yard sale, don't be discouraged if it's not in perfect shape. Use the good parts to make a pillow. Plump pillows are especially sumptuous, so we made the pillow covering somewhat smaller than the pillow form.

1. If your bedspread has fringe, carefully cut out the stitches and remove the fringe. Cut the fringe into two pieces, 21 inches long each.

2. Pin together the two pieces of fabric, right sides facing. Machine stitch a 1/2-inch seam allowance around all sides, leaving a 10-inch gap in a short end to insert the pillow. Remove the pins. Press.

3. Turn the case right side out. Pin one strip of fringe across the seamed short end, turning the fringe under itself 1 1/2 inches at each end for a neat edge. Hand sew the fringe to the fabric with closely spaced running stitches (see Techniques). Remove the pins.

4. Insert the pillow, then sew closed the opening with slip stitches (see Techniques). Attach the remaining fringe to the other side as you did the first.

standard size down-filled bed pillow

two 19 x 21 1/2-inch pieces chenille (from an old bedspread)

42 inches fringe (optional)

❖   ❖   ❖

tartan pillow

These cheery Stewart tartan pillows, with their robust coloring, were created out of a kilt salvaged from a secondhand store. They are trimmed with a self-fringe border. When working with plaids, or any fabric with a strong stripe or pattern, you will need to match up the lines of the design; to do this, you may need slightly more fabric than if you were working with a solid color.

1. Cut two identical 12-inch-square pieces of fabric, one for the front, one for the back. When selecting your fabric, keep in mind that every plaid is different in its repeat, and that you will need enough fabric to get two identical squares. Use a 12-inch square paper pattern to "preview" the plaid: Fold the fabric in half so that the horizontal and vertical lines of the plaid match up. Pin. Starting from the folded edge, locate the center of the repeat of the plaid and pin the paper pattern accordingly, about ¹/₂ inch from the fold. Cut out two pieces and remove the pins.

2. Pin together the two fabric pieces. (The tartan is probably identical on both sides. If not, pin the wrong sides together.) Double machine stitch a 2-inch seam allowance all around, leaving a 6-inch gap to insert the pillow form. Remove the pins.

3. Insert the pillow form and securely sew closed the opening with a running stitch. If you are adding a decorative braid to hide the machine stitching, pin it all around the pillow over the seamed stitches. Tuck each end in under itself, for a neat finish. With matching thread, hand sew the braid to the pillow with tiny stitches.

4. To make the self-fringe border, starting with the corner of the outer edge, pull the first horizontal thread from the material all the way across the border. Repeat until the desired width of fringe is reached. Use the same method for the remaining three sides.

❖   ❖   ❖

LARGE SQUARE PILLOW:

10-inch pillow form

¹/₂ yard tartan wool (or more depending on repeat)

50 inches braid (optional)

vintage fabrics

Linking the past with the present, pillows made from pieces of vintage fabrics can give any decor, traditional or contemporary, a warm personal feeling. By reworking

interesting patterns, antique trimmings, and eccentric colors, you can add personality and a whole new spin to a room. Even better, by using materials with a history to them, you're the author of a dynamic new chapter in their lives.

Finding vintage fabrics

For those of us fortunate enough to inherit old pieces—Great-Grandmother's embroidered handkerchiefs, Aunt Ellie's table runners—we can create pillows rich in family nostalgia. Lacking that resource, we can always invent a pedigree with forays to antiques shops, estate sales, flea markets, consignment shops, and thrift shops. In my own experience, church rummage sales are a gold mine, yielding vast rewards for those willing to dig deep.

Never overlook the torn or worn—you may fall in love with the vivid color of a battered silk curtain, but shy away because of its condition. But it's a rare object that doesn't have some portion worth salvaging. Something that has outgrown its original use may still have beautiful parts. A friend who sews lovely wedding trousseaux makes her best bolster pillows from old hotel linens by artfully cutting and rearranging the good parts. An entire collection of pillows can be created from vintage handkerchiefs—especially those boldly patterned ones of the 1930s and 1940s—perhaps cut into strips of different lengths and widths and stitched together.

When on the search for special discoveries, don't limit yourself by looking at only a few types of things. You can never think too small. Your imagination can be increased by

In an old Mississippi farmhouse, feed sacks made of white muslin become a stunning, oversize pillow to dress the bed (above).

A piece of vintage fabric discovered by a California collector is stitched up into a simple square pillow (opposite).

exercise—look at old jackets, shirts, and blouses in addition to the more obvious tablecloths, linens, and patchwork quilts. I love to buy old velvet dresses—the velvet is so much richer than anything available today. I cut out the good parts for ruffles and borders. Before making your purchase, turn the item inside out to see if there is enough area between the seams to use for your project. The Tartan Pillows pictured on page 85 were made with fabric from an over-the-hill kilt.

Quilts are a beloved source for pillows. While there is a school of thought that believes no quilt should ever be taken apart, some quilts are so worn that it seems a shame to pass them by at the flea market or, worse, discard them. If a quilt is torn or ripped, rescue it for its blocks. Transform the blocks into pillows by seaming along their outer edges. If they are truly antique pieces, display the pillows in out-of-the-way places where they will not suffer too much wear-and-tear. Make good use of small pieces of vintage fabrics by creating your own quilt pillow. A patchwork design—with its same-size squares of colorful fabrics—is the easiest to assemble but there

are many, many quilt patterns and templates available that can easily be adapted for a pillow. Find a pattern that has a strong block design and make just as many of them as you need for your desired pillow size.

When shopping, always keep in mind the Accessory Factor. You may run across an object that looks totally shot and wonder how on earth someone could be selling such a thing. But a closer inspection may reveal hidden treasure—a set of leather-covered buttons, perfect for a houndstooth wool pillow; a tasseled fringe to border small sachets; or a regal-looking crest on a blazer pocket that would look spectacular on a velvet

Sewing on vintage lace personalizes these store-bought pillowcases (opposite) and makes for a lovely wedding gift. A collection of quilt pillows—some made from rescued quilt blocks, some made from fabric scraps expressly as pillows—livens up a guest bedroom (right).

pillow. Look for details: tassels, old buttons, frog closings, braids and rope borders, embroidered ribbon. By spotting these small, powerful design elements, you will assemble a trimmings and accessories collection that will be far more personal than anything from a shop shelf.

If you find a piece of fabric that is particularly appealing but particularly distressed, appliqué the good part onto a larger pillow. With the Sunflower Appliquéd Circle (page 19), we rescued a motif from a favorite piece of old fabric and cut away the damaged areas, leaving a bold image. Vintage fabrics of the 1940s and 1950s tend to feature such strong patterns. Botanical prints and drawings have beautiful detail and subtle color, and if you can't find a vintage pattern, you may be able to find one of the many reproductions now available.

Preparing antique linens and cottons for sewing

If the linens are precious or valuable, before trying to remove stains you should consult a fabric conservator. If they simply need freshening, you may launder them the way Victorian housekeepers did. In *Beeton's Book of Household Management*, published in 1861,

In an old house full of antiques, even the pillows fit in: A needlepoint pillow (left) beckons a visitor to sit for a while. The exquisite piece of handiwork was sewn to a gold velvet backing; tassels and braid add a luxurious touch. Large pillows stitched from vintage brocade and trimmed with complementary tassels and fringe play off a velvet patchwork country quilt (right).

the author, Mrs. Isabella Beeton, instructs that "coloured muslins, cottons, and linens should be put into cold water and washed very speedily, using common yellow soap, which should be rinsed off immediately. When washed thoroughly, they should be rinsed in succession in soft water, in which common salt has been dissolved, in the proportion of a handful to three or four gallons, and afterwards wrung gently, as soon as rinsed, with as little twisting as possible, and then hung out to dry. Delicate-coloured articles should not be exposed to the sun, but dried in the shade, using clean lines and wooden pegs."

If you're using silks, you may be interested to know that Mrs. Beeton advised, "Silks, when washed, should be dried in the shade, on a linen-horse, taking care that they are kept smooth and unwrinkled; if old and rusty, a pint of common spirits should be mixed with each gallon of water. Satin and silk ribbons, both white and coloured, may be cleaned in the same manner."

While some vintage materials can be hand-washed, rare or costly pieces should have expert attention. Many antiques dealers who specialize in vintage clothing, trims, and accessories are willing to give advice on fabric care. Magazines are another source for learning about fabrics: Newsstands are flooded with magazines devoted to antiques,

Victoriana, and folk art. If you want to research back issues, most likely your library can direct you to the magazine's articles index, where you can learn more about the proper care of such valuables. Other sources

of help are the textile departments of local colleges and museums. I've found local historical societies to be gold mines of reliable information concerning the care of fabrics and trimmings.

Tea-staining

The opposite idea of using vintage fabrics is to age new fabrics to fit in with old. Tea-staining is a popular technique for toning down the too-new look of many cotton prints or muslins. One method for doing this is to brew a pot of strong tea by placing a dozen or so tea bags in a tea pot and filling the pot with boiling water. Let the tea steep for at least 10 minutes. Place a stopper in the bottom of a kitchen sink, arrange fabric as flat as possible and pour the tea mixture over the fabric. With a wooden spoon, lift the fabric, adjusting it to evenly distribute the tea. After allowing the fabric to sit for 15 to 20 minutes, gently wring out the excess tea. Once the stain is set, the fabric can be laundered with a mild detergent to mask any tea scent.

On a sun-dappled porch, a gently worn pillow cut from a piece of old tapestry softens a rustic swing. Two smaller throw pillows sit nearby, ready to greet someone seeking a quiet moment.

chapter five

materials & techniques

One of the joys of sewing is that it is an ancient art that requires little in the way of complicated equipment. In crafting pillows this is especially true. Given their relatively small sizes, most pillows can easily be hand sewn. Indeed, as we've shown, there are even a few that require no sewing at all.

But whether or not you use a sewing machine, there are certain techniques that make any sewing project easier, and the end product more finished looking.

Throughout this book, a range of handmade pillows have been provided, from super-easy to more advanced options that have details, trimmings, appliqués, or zippers. Whatever the scope of the project, there are certain tools of the trade that are necessary to pillow-making, along with standard sewing techniques—and this chapter is devoted to the basics. Most of the materials discussed here can be assembled with a trip to a good sewing or craft store. Many things you probably have at home already. Remember, with sewing, as with any other craft, it always pays to use high quality goods. Treat yourself to the best.

equipment

While you may be able to hand sew most pillows, things certainly go more quickly with a sewing machine. Years ago, my mother introduced all her daughters to the joys of the Singer Featherweight, a compact, portable sewing machine that, despite its delicate appearance, is a tireless workhorse. It has everything you need: It sews even, perfect stitches, threads easily, and is a breeze to operate. Many people adore the new electronic sewing machines, which offer a staggering variety of stitches and attachments, such as rufflers, zigzaggers, and edge stitchers. For the sake of simplicity, all the projects in this book were made without any special attachments other than a zipper foot, which allows you to sew close to either the right or left side of a zipper.

High up on the list of sewing necessities is a steam iron. Seams that are pressed flat during the process of making a pillow, rather than at its completion, make the fabric lay better and give the pillow a much more finished appearance. Keep your iron clean—if it has rust spots or leaks water, it may damage your work. Press as you go along, and if you are working on cotton, linen, canvas, organdy, or oxford cloth, it's also worth using a light spray starch. This will help keep the seams very flat so that when you make joints everything is smooth and in place. Press the fabric on the wrong side, or use a cloth on the right side to protect its surface.

Everyone who sews has their favorite tools. Among mine is a really sharp pair of pinking shears. I use these to pink nearly all fabric edges to prevent fraying, and occasionally to cut felt. Unfortunately, felt can dull scissors so it's recommended that your best scissors be used sparingly with this fabric.

A sharp pair of medium-size dressmaker's scissors is indispensable. Personal feel and fit are paramount here. Scissors that are overly heavy are tiring to work with; if they're overly long, it's difficult to make a clean cut. Keep these scissors solely for cutting fabric. Also have on hand a pair of general-purpose scissors for cutting paper or templates. A utility knife or X-Acto knife is good for cutting cardboard.

Measuring tools are among the most critical sewing tools. Accurate measurements in sewing, as in baking, can spell the difference between success and disaster. At one time, wooden yardsticks were routinely given away in fabric stores. The better stores still offer this service. Along with a yardstick, you'll need a foot-long ruler. A plastic T-square is very useful for marking accurately. A fabric tape measure lets you calculate the circumference of objects such as pillow forms. A compass makes precise circles—just be sure it doesn't slip out of the measurement as so many of the inexpensive compasses made for school children can do.

If you're organized enough to have an actual sewing kit, or are putting one together now, make sure there's a place for a pin box filled with stainless steel dressmaking pins. Quality pays off here: Steel won't rust and stain your material. Pins with bright plastic heads are wonderful—they're easy to spot if you've forgotten to remove them. An assortment of different size and different purpose needles should be included. If you plan to make the Cross-Stitch Pillow (page 54), you'll find an embroidery needle makes cleaner stitches. If you make your own pincushion (page 38), you'll never go hunting for your favorite needles again and they won't become dull.

The thimble, it seems, has almost gone the way of the calling card. It's a loss because a thimble can help one sew quickly by pushing the needle through thick seams. Sewing with a thimble does take practice, but once you learn, you'll probably never do without one.

To mark your fabric, special pencils make removable marks, as does dressmaker's chalk. On light fabrics, use lead or blue pencil; white chalk or pencil is best for dark colors.

Some people like to keep spools of thread in a separate thread box so they don't unwind and get messy. Match the color thread to the fabric—and if you're sewing a few different colors, match the thread to the darkest color you are sewing. If you need a neutral color, gray or beige are best. The weight and type of thread should also match the fabric. Synthetic fabrics need polyester threads; heavier materials, such as pieces of old rugs and textiles, should probably be hand sewn with heavier cotton threads. General all-purpose threads are readily available and will suit most projects.

A box in your sewing kit with lots of extra bobbins for the sewing machine is a time saver; few things are as frustrating as unwinding the thread from a bobbin because you can't find an empty one.

Of course all of us hope not to make any mistakes, but if you do, you'll need a seam ripper, which will also come in handy if you work with vintage fabrics and need to remove a section of lace or trim.

fabrics

Most fabrics that you will buy come in measurements of 36, 45, or 60 inches wide. Unless stated otherwise, the instructions in this book assume you have a fabric that is at least 45 inches wide.

A complex and exciting world of fabric options exists for the pillow maker. In this book, we've included a range of familiar fabrics: felt, oxford cloth, chintz, gingham, dotted Swiss, and linen. Along with these, we've added some twists by using familiar materials in new ways: the woven strip pillow and pillows covered in bandanas. And we've explored some of the other-than-fabric choices for pillows: bedspreads, ribbons. But whatever material you select, the material needs to be prepared for pillow making.

Start with absolutely clean material. If purchasing new material, be sure to ask the salesperson what the fabric content is and how to care for it. Unlike finished goods, fabric does not come with a label, so it's up to the individual to learn more about it—whether it shrinks, whether it's colorfast, etc. Always purchase extra if you think the fabric may shrink and you plan to remove the pillow cover for laundering.

If you wish to freshen up cotton, linen, silk, wool, or muslin, they can be laundered at home, in a mild detergent (see Vintage Fabrics, page 90). If possible, hang them on a clothesline to dry in order to avoid prolonged exposure to heat in a clothes dryer. With blended or synthetic fabrics, it's safest to consult a good dry cleaner if you need to remove stains.

Whatever the material you select, it must be crease- and wrinkle-free before measuring and cutting. Follow the instructions on your iron for the correct setting before pressing. Once ironed, place the material unfolded on a flat surface. Before measuring and cutting, be sure the fabric is straight. Large cutting boards, made from heavy cardboard imprinted with measurements, are valuable time savers for this. If you lack one, make sure the fabric appears straight and double-check with a ruler before cutting.

If you are using a fabric with a design, you'll need to buy enough so that you can get the pattern to match. Matching a design for a pillow usually is simply a matter of matching up the front panel to the back. If the fabric has a repeat, center the motif in the middle of both pieces. If it is striped or plaid, be sure the

design falls in the same position in each piece. As mentioned in the instructions for the Tartan Pillow (page 85), you may wish to make a paper pattern to preview your options before cutting. Try using a paper that is not too opaque, such as tracing paper or waxed paper, and cut it to the size required.

Some fabrics, such as velvet or corduroy, have a nap, which means that if you brush the surface of the fabric one way, it appears lighter and shinier than if you brush it the other way. Decide which look you like best, then cut all pieces of fabric with the top edges facing the same direction.

To mark your fabric before measuring, use a pencil or dressmaker's chalk in a contrasting color. If pinning on a pattern, use steel pins. (Try not to leave them in for long periods as they can make permanent holes in some fabrics.) If possible, cut the fabric in the same direction for uniformity. Keep the fabric flat if your work is interrupted, and always press as you go.

forms and fillings

Ready-made pillow forms are available in craft and sewing stores in a variety of sizes and shapes, and with different fillings. By far, the most common filling is a polyester fiber filling. This can be quite stiff and give a good form to a pillow. Pillow forms made from a fifty-fifty mix of feathers and down are expensive, but they give a pillow a soft luxury like no other filling. An all-down pillow, however, is actually too much of a good thing: It is too soft to be useful.

The filling itself can influence what form to choose: A floppy down-stuffed pillow would probably be best in an oblong or square shape, for example. A circle form needs a firmer form to hold its shape.

The ever-popular ready-made square sizes available are 10, 12, and 14 inches. We made our Oversize Reading Pillow (page 25) from a 24-inch square. The classic bolster form, so useful for a daybed, is available in different sizes; 6 x 17 inches is one standard. Circle pillows commonly come in diameters of 8 inches and up. One shape that is not used nearly enough is the triangle. Triangles impart a note of formality, especially to chairs and chaise longues. The rectangle is enormously versatile; it can be as an arm rest, a sofa back, or a bed pillow with equal success.

If you can't find a pillow form in the shape you want, make your own. Both polyester and cotton batting are available in sheets of different thicknesses as well as loose in bags. Using plain cotton fabric or muslin, cut out and sew a pillow in the form you desire, leaving a gap on one side for filling. Stuff to the plumpness you prefer, then sew up

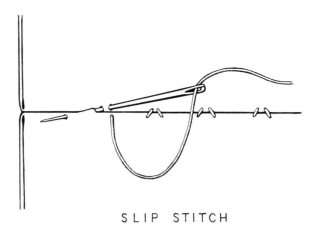

SLIP STITCH

the open end with slip stitches. Foam blocks, also available in different thicknesses and densities, can be covered using the same method.

stitches

There are basically two types of stitches: utility stitches to hold things together—basting, gathering, and sewing stitches—and decorative stitches sewn on the surface of material.

Among the basic utility stitches, we use the slip stitch (see Illustration) to close up many of our pillows because it's a stitch that holds together two folded edges well, is almost invisible, and is easily removed for laundering the pillowcase. Pin together the two fabric edges and, working from the right to the left, insert a needle and thread through the bottom piece close to the folded edge. Pick up a thread or two from the top piece of fabric, then insert the needle back into the bottom folded edge, slipping it through the fold about $1/8$ inch along. Bring the needle out and pull thread through. Continue until

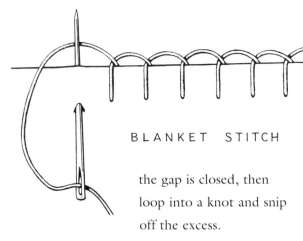

BLANKET STITCH

the gap is closed, then loop into a knot and snip off the excess.

When you want to put your own stamp on a project, especially when it's a simple shape, a decoration of embroidered stitches couldn't be prettier. Fortunately, there is an extensive vocabulary of decorative stitches handed down through time to inspire you. Up until this century, needlework was a much cherished art, an important part of a young girl's education. Samplers were patiently sewn stitch by stitch as a way to both develop and display one's skills. Samplers also served another purpose; they recorded new stitches and were referred to when a girl needed to remember how a stitch was made. Today, of course, we have printed embroidery books with instructions. But the stitches remain the same.

A nice, simple decorative stitch that can be learned quickly is the blanket stitch (see Illustration). We finished the edges of our Felt Christmas Pillow (page 43) with this stitch, which is a variation on the buttonhole stitch. The old-fashioned blanket stitch prevents fabric from fraying and adds a colorful edge to a pillow. Although this stitch can be sewn with any thread, blanket stitches are associated with heavier yarns and embroidery flosses. If that's what you plan, use a heavier needle with a larger eye opening. Working from right to left, start the stitch by inserting a needle with a knotted thread through the back, about 1/2 inch from edge. Insert the needle back through the fabric covering the previous stitch but leaving a loop. Insert the needle through this loop and pull at the top. Now to make a row of stitches, insert needle from the front to the back, again at the 1/2-inch distance from the edge, and spaced apart from the first stitch however much you want (1/2 inch is traditional). Before pulling the needle through, carry the thread under the point of the needle making a loop as shown in the illustration. Work the entire row making sure the height and distance of the stitches is consistent.

There are many different hemming stitches that can be used to secure a folded edge. One basic hemming stitch leaves tiny stitches on the right side of the fabric. (If hemming is new to you, it's best to practice so that the finished hem has consistently sized and spaced stitches.) On the wrong side of the fabric, fold in a hem to the allowance you desire and pin. We like to stitch with the pinned hem facing toward us. Using a needle with a long piece of knotted thread, insert the needle under the folded hem close to the edge, then bring it down and pick up a few threads from the flat fabric. With the needle pointing diagonally, from right to left, slide it up under the folded edge about $1/4$ inch away, then bring it up through the fold. Repeat until finished.

Basting stitches are invaluable for holding fabric in place, especially before permanently machine stitching together. Some fabrics, such as silk and organdy, which are slippery, really need basting stitches, while other fabrics stick together well, like velvet and felt. Usually, basting stitches are removed at the end of a project. A basting stitch consists of a series of long evenly sized running stitches, usually $1/4$- to $3/8$-inch long. Take three horizontal stitches at a time on your needle, "running" along the seam line of your fabric or wherever you wish to baste. Then pull the thread through and repeat until finished. Knot the thread.

Gathering stitches are used to make ruffles, to ease fabric around corners, or to close up circles. Gathering stitches can be made on many sewing machines, or by hand. To hand stitch gathers, simply take a needle with a very long piece of knotted thread and make a series of basting stitches along the length of the piece you want to gather. Leave the thread unknotted, then with another threaded needle repeat this stitch in a row close to and parallel to the first one. When you reach the end, pull both threads gently to make even gathers and knot the threads securely to hold the gathers in place.

seams

Dressmakers use many different types of seams—the line formed when two pieces of fabric are stitched together. (A seam allowance is the strip of fabric left after a seam has been stitched, to allow for fraying. A hem is created when fabric is turned down along its edge.) For our purposes, a simple plain seam is the most versatile. If you put the time into making proper seams, it will pay off handsomely in the finished appearance of your pillow. First, you should always lay your fabric down on a flat surface and smooth the two raw edges together until they match perfectly. Pin and, if necessary, baste, usually $3/8$ inch away from the edge. (Since most basting stitches are removed afterward, never machine stitch over the basting line.) Place the pinned or basted fabric under the presser foot and stitch a straight seam with the allowance you wish ($5/8$ and $1/2$ inch being two standard allowances) and make a few back stitches at each end for extra security. You may trim any extra bulk with pinking shears or regular scissors.

If working with a cloth that frays easily, such as organza or some polyesters, you could sew a clean-stitched seam. This is made by turning under each edge of the seam $1/8$ inch and stitching close to the edge.

To ease the fit of a pillow with curved seams, you can trim them down. There are two types of curved seams: convex and concave. Convex seams are those that are outward facing. Cut a series of small, evenly spaced slits in the seam allowance, being careful not to go into the stitching. To help ease inward facing concave seams, remove tiny bits of the fabric by making a series of shallow notches about one inch apart in the seam allowance.

closures

Before you choose a pillow closure, consider the type of fabric you are working with, and the kind of pillow you are making. Are you using a vintage fabric or other delicate cloth

that you will not want to wash? Do you intend to put the pillow in a child's room, where it is sure to get dirty, or is it merely for display, to be placed on a chair in a corner? Your answers will determine whether or not you make a pillow cover that can be removed.

If you do not expect to wash the pillow cover, you do not need to make a removable one. In this case, closing up the seam with slipstitches after you have inserted the pillow form is a perfectly acceptable option (as in the Woven Shaker Pillow, page 41). And if you change your mind and do want to launder the cover, slip stitches are easy to remove with a seam ripper.

There are numerous options for a removable pillow cover. Among the most common are closing the back of a cover with a simple overflap, or using buttons or a zipper to keep the pillow in its case.

The overlap closure (as in the Lace Sham, page 49) is one of the easiest closures to make. The simplest way to make one is to cut two sections of fabric for the back that are a bit wider than you need. Make the hems, overlap the sections, then trim away any excess fabric, so that the pillow back is exactly the same size as the front.

Buttons can be both decorative as well as practical. You can display a collection of old buttons as a design element (as in the

Buttoned-Up Square, page 17) as well as a closure on a pillow front, or use buttons to close an overlap on the back.

Zippers are the least visible of closures. They can either be inserted across the center of the pillow back, or along the edge of a seam (see the Country Check Pillow, page 37). Buy a zipper in a color that matches your fabric. A zipper foot on a sewing machine makes putting in a zipper an easy exercise.

A sophisticated closure option for a pillowcase is to keep the edges open but to attach two or three tassels, or a few pretty ribbons, along the edge to keep the pillow inside the cover.

finishings

Attaching trimmings requires careful pinning and, in most cases, hand stitching. If you are adding a braid or trim of the type that unravels, cover both raw ends with a little Scotch tape. If the trim is flat, pin it all the way around, allowing an inch or more for overlapping where the two ends meet. Carefully sew on the trim with a series of small even stitches. At the end, remove the tape, fold over the extra trim, and attach securely.

When attaching a rounded trim, such as cording, another technique for concealing the ends is to bury them in the pillow seam. Allow an extra inch or so to your trim measurement. When sewing up the pillow seam, leave a 1-inch section open. Into this opening, insert one end of the trimming, pushing it down about $1/2$ inch. Pin on the remaining trim around the pillow, and when finished, insert the other end of the trimming, pushing it into the opening, also about $1/2$ inch down. Attach with small stitches while closing the opening.

Accenting the color, line, shape, and texture of pillows, trimmings have personality to spare. Braid can enliven a somber material, piping makes a tailored silhouette, and tassels provide style. A deep fringe falls with abandon, a traditional ball fringe just about dances. Adapt the Ruffled Chintz Bolster (page 27) by sewing on a long tassel instead of a ruffle, and the pillow

becomes very extroverted. Buttons seem lighthearted, as do bows and tufts.

More than just adding panache, trimming serves a practical purpose; it conceals seams in a most handsome way. Ribbon, cording, braid, and fringe are available in many styles, sizes, widths, thicknesses, and colors—and in many price ranges. Other trims come with a woven edge that is meant to be machine sewn directly into the seam for a very defined shape. Decorative trims with woven edges are sewn on just like piping.

If you wish to make your own piping, start by purchasing cording from a sewing store. Cording comes in different sizes; choose the thickness you want, calculating how much you need to extend around the perimeter of the pillow. Tape the ends with Scotch tape so that they don't unravel.

Most piping is made from strips cut on the bias for greater flexibility. Ready-made bias tape is available in a limited range of colors, but in most instances, you'll cut out your own bias strips. Take a square of fabric, usually 12 inches or more, and fold it in half diagonally. The diagonal is called the bias line. Cut the material in half on the bias line to make two triangles. Using a ruler and dressmaker's chalk, mark off a series of evenly spaced lines parallel to the bias line, according to the width you want for the piping. We like

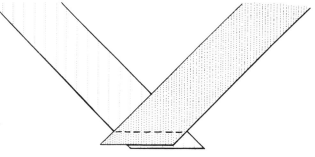

to add the width of the cording to 1½ inches of fabric (a ¾-inch seam allowance). Cut out the strips and join by placing the right sides together at the short ends and pinning. The strip will have a V shape (see Illustration). Machine stitch and press seams open. Trim the little corners so that the strip is continuous. When you have enough bias stripping stitched together to reach around the perimeter of the pillow, plus 1 inch for an overlap, fold the right side of the bias stripping in half lengthwise over the cording. At the end with the 1-inch overlap, fold the right side of the fabric in ½ inch to make a finished end. Pin and machine stitch lengthwise close to the cording. (A zipper foot is very useful here.)

To attach the piping to your pillow, pin the raw edge of the piping along the seam line in between the front and back panels, which are wrong side out. Where the piping ends meet, tuck the raw edge inside the ½-inch overlap. Stitch across the joint. Attach the entire piping either by hand basting or by machine stitching.

resources

ALLIED DOWN
84 Oak Street
Brooklyn, NY 11222
(718) 389-5454
fabric, ticking, fillings

B&J FABRICS
263 West 40th Street
New York, NY 10018
(212) 354-8150
raw silk by the yard

BECKENSTEIN'S LADIES FABRICS
125 Orchard Street
Box 1056
New York, NY 10002
(212) 475-7575
raw silk by the yard

BENNISON FABRICS
76 Greene Street
New York, NY 10012
(212) 941-1212
fabric

THE BUTTON GALLERY
2283 Business Way
Riverside, CA 92501-2246
(800) 287-6275
buttons

CALICO CORNERS
(98 locations)
(800) 213-6366
fabric and trimmings

COCONUT COMPANY
131 Greene Street
New York, NY 10012
(212) 539-1940
fabric

COUNTRY STITCHING
P.O. Box 119
Willow Grove, PA 19090
(215) 699-8170
sampler kits

CRAFT KING
P.O. Box 90637
Lakeland, FL 33804
(800) 769-9494
ribbons, fillings, laces, trim

CUDDLEDOWN OF MAINE
Freeport, Maine
(888) 235-3696
http: //www.cuddledown.com
handmade down pillows

DOWN DECOR
1910 South Street
Cincinnati, OH 45204
(800) 792-3696
feather and down fillings

ECONOMY FOAM
& FUTON CO.
173 East Houston Street
New York, NY 10002
(212) 473-4462
pillow forms

HYMAN HENDLER & SONS
67 West 38th Street
New York, NY 10018
(212) 840-8393
ribbons, tassels, braids

WILLIAM ITZKOWITZ
174 Ludlow Street
New York, NY 10002
(212) 477-1788
pillow forms

M&J TRIMMING
1014 Sixth Avenue
New York, NY 10018
(212) 391-8731
trim

NANCY'S SEWING BASKET
2221 Queen Anne Avenue N.
Seattle, WA 98109
(206) 282-9112
**ribbons, pillow forms, new
and antique trims**

PILLOW FINERY
979 Third Avenue
New York, NY 10022
(212) 752-9603
fillings

P&S FABRIC
355 Broadway
New York, NY 10013
(212) 226-1534
fabric

JEWELL SCHRANG
Quail Country Antiques
1581 Boulevard Way
Walnut Creek, CA 94595
(510) 944-0930
ticking

SHAKER WORKSHOPS
P.O. Box 8001
Ashburnham, MA 10430
(800) 840-9121
Shaker canvas chair tape

SILK SURPLUS ANNEX
223 East 58th Street
New York, NY 10022
(212) 759-1294
velvet by the yard

STEINLAUF & STOLLER, INC.
239 West 39th Street
New York, NY 10018
(212) 869-0321
fillings

THE STITCHERY
120 North Meadows Road
Medfield, MA 02052
(508) 359-7702
cross-stitch supplies

TREADLEART
25834 Narbonne Avenue
Lomita, CA 90717
(310) 534-5122
http://www.treadleart.com
needles, thread

index

Entries and page numbers in bold refer to individual pillow instructions.

Acknowledgments

The author would like to thank:

Pillow Finery

Shaker Workshops

Chris Stone & Associates

J.B. Martin Co., Inc.

Many thanks to Mecox Gardens, Southampton, New York.